The Art of Saving

How to budget and save money each month

By **Faith Poulter**

CONTENTS

Introduction   05

Chapter I   07
Understanding your finances

Chapter II   15
Establishing a budget

Chapter III   21
Effective saving techniques

Chapter IV   24
Maintaining and adjusting the budget

Chapter V   27
Tips and tricks to maximize savings

Conclusion   30

Additional Resources   32

INTRODUCTION

EFFECTIVE FINANCIAL MANAGEMENT AND DISCIPLINED SAVING HABITS ARE THE CORNERSTONES OF A SECURE AND PROSPEROUS FUTURE.

Saving money is not just about putting aside a portion of your income; it's about creating a financial buffer that provides peace of mind and the ability to handle unexpected expenses. Proper financial management enables you to control your spending, reduce debt, and make informed decisions about your financial future. By mastering these skills, you can achieve your financial goals and enjoy a higher quality of life.

Objective of the Book

The essential objective of this book is to supply you with practical and effective strategies to set up and take after a budget, in this manner maximizing your investment funds each month. This direct is outlined to be clear and significant, advertising step-by-step instructions on how to oversee your accounts proficiently.

Whether you're fair beginning your budgetary travel or looking to move forward your existing monetary procedures, this book points to prepare you with the information and apparatuses fundamental to require control of your monetary predetermination.

What to anticipate by the conclusion of the book

By the conclusion of this book, you'll anticipate to have a comprehensive understanding of budgeting and sparing strategies. You'll learn how to:

- **Make an Viable Budget**: Create a reasonable and maintainable budget custom-made to your wage and costs.
- **Track and Control Your Investing**: Actualize techniques to screen your investing propensities and maintain a strategic distance from pointless uses.
- **Diminish and Oversee Obligation**: Get it distinctive sorts of obligation and learn strategies to pay them off productively.
- **Set and Accomplish Monetary Goals**: Characterize clear monetary goals and make a arrange to attain them.
- **Utilize Money related Instruments and Assets**: Investigate different devices and assets accessible to help you in overseeing your accounts successfully.

CHAPTER I

UNDERSTANDING YOUR FINANCES

Assessing Your Current Money related Circumstance

The primary step in acing your funds is to completely assess your current monetary circumstance. This includes taking a nitty gritty see at your resources, liabilities, salary, and costs. Begin by posting all your resources, which incorporate cash, reserve funds, speculations, property, and any other resources you possess. Another, list your liabilities, such as exceptional obligations, advances, credit card equalizations, and other budgetary commitments. The distinction between your resources and liabilities is your net worth, which gives a depiction of your monetary wellbeing.

Understanding your net worth makes a difference you see where you stand monetarily and sets the arrange for creating a comprehensive budget. Frequently overhauling this assessment will empower you to track your budgetary advance and make vital alterations to your budgetary arrange.

Identifying Income and Expenses

Precisely recognizing your salary and costs is pivotal for compelling money related administration.

Start by calculating your add up to month to month pay, counting your compensation, rewards, independent work, rental pay, and any other sources of income. It is basic to account for both settled and variable earnings to urge a total picture of your budgetary inflows.

Another, categorize your costs into settled and variable costs. Settled costs are those that stay steady each month, such as lease or contract installments, utility bills, and protections premiums. Variable costs vacillate from month to month and incorporate foodstuffs, amusement, eating out, and other optional investing.

By breaking down your expenses into these categories, you will be able better understand where your cash is going and distinguish ranges where you will cut back or alter your investing. This step is basic for making a practical and successful budget.

Tools for recording and analyzing your finances

To manage your finances effectively, it is important to use tools that help you record and analyze your financial data. Here are some popular options:

- **Spreadsheets**: Programs like Microsoft Excel and Google Sheets are powerful tools for tracking income and expenses. You can create custom templates to suit your needs, and these tools often come with built-in functions for calculating totals and generating reports.

- **Budgeting Apps**: Numerous mobile apps are designed to help you track your finances on the go. Apps like Mint, YNAB (You Need A Budget), and Pocket Guard allow you to link your bank accounts, categorize expenses, set financial goals, and receive alerts about your spending habits.
- **Financial Software:** Comprehensive monetary management software such as Quicken or Personal Capital offers advanced features for tracking investments, planning budgets, and analyzing your overall financial situation. These tools often provide detailed reports and insights to help you make informed decisions.
- **Paper Journals:** For those who prefer a more traditional approach, maintaining a written journal can be effective. Using a dedicated finance journal, you can manually record your income, expenses, and financial goals. This method can be particularly useful for individuals who enjoy the tactile experience of writing things down and reviewing them physically.

Using these tools, you will pick up a clearer understanding of your money related circumstance and make more educated choices around your cash. Whether you incline toward advanced arrangements or conventional strategies, the key is consistency in following and analyzing your accounts. By completely assessing your money related circumstance, precisely recognizing your pay and expenses, and utilizing compelling instruments, you will lay a solid establishment for fruitful money related administration. This understanding is pivotal as you move forward in your travel to budgeting and sparing viably, guaranteeing that you simply have a clear and practical picture of your money related scene.

Evaluating your current financial situation
A practical example

Evaluating your current financial situation is the first and most crucial step in gaining control over your finances. Here is a step-by-step example to help you understand how to perform this evaluation:

Step 1: List Your Assets

Start by listing all your assets. Assets are anything of value that you own. Include:
- **Cash and Bank Accounts**: Check the balances in your checking and savings accounts.
- **Investments**: List the value of stocks, bonds, mutual funds, and retirement accounts.
- **Real Estate**: Include the current market value of any property you own.
- **Personal Property**: Consider valuable items such as cars, jewelry, or art.
- **Other Assets**: Include any other assets, such as business ownership or collectibles.

Example:

Asset Type	Value
Checking Account:	$3,000
Savings Account:	$5,000
Retirement Account:	$25,000
Stocks	$10,000
Car	$8,000
Home Market Value	$150,000
Total Assets:	$201,000

Step 2: List Your Liabilities

Next, list all your liabilities. Liabilities are debts or financial obligations you owe. Include:

- **Credit Card Debt:** List the outstanding balances on all credit cards.
- **Loans:** Include personal loans, student loans, auto loans, and mortgages.
- **Other Debts:** Include any other debts, such as medical bills or lines of credit.

Example:

Liability type	Amount owed
Credit Card Debt	$2,000
Student Loan	$15,000
Auto Loan	$5,000
Mortgage	$120,000
Total liabilities:	**$142,000**

Step 3: Calculate Your Net Worth

Subtract your total liabilities from your total assets to determine your net worth.

Example:

	Amount
Total Assets	$201,000
Total liabilities	$142,000
Net Worth:	**$59,000**

Your **net worth** provides a snapshot of your overall financial health. A positive net worth indicates that your assets exceed your liabilities, while a negative net worth indicates that you owe more than you own.

Step 4: Track Your Income

List all sources of your monthly income. Include:

- **Salary:** Take-home pay after taxes and other deductions.
- **Side Income:** Income from freelance work, part-time jobs, or other sources.
- **Investment Income:** Dividends, interest, or rental income.
- **Other Income:** Any other regular income sources.

Example:

Income Source	Monthly Amount
Salary	$3,500
Freelance Work	$500
Rental Income	$600
Total Monthly Income:	**$4,600**

Step 5: Track Your Expenses

List all your monthly expenses. Categorize them into fixed and variable expenses.

Example:

Expense Type	Monthly Amount
Fixed expenses	
Rent/Mortgage	$1,200
Utilities	$150
Insurance	$200
Loan Payments	$400
Total Fixed Expenses	**$1,950**
Variable expenses	
Groceries	$400
Transportation	$150
Entertainment	$100
Dining Out	$150
Miscellaneous	$100
Total Variable Expenses	**$900**
Total Monthly Expenses	**$2,850**

Step 6: Analyze Your Cash Flow

Calculate your month-to-month cash stream by subtracting your add up to costs from your add up to wage.

Example:

	Amount
Total Monthly Income	$4,600
Total Monthly Expenses	$2,850
Monthly Cash Flow:	$1,750

A **positive cash** stream implies you have money left over each month, which you will utilize for savings, ventures, or paying down obligation. A **negative cash** flow indicates merely are investing more than you gain, and you will get to alter your budget or discover extra pay sources.

Step 7: Create a Financial Summary

Summarize your discoveries to urge a clear picture of your current monetary circumstance:

Example:

Financial Summary	Amount
Total Assets	$201,000
Total Liabilities	$142,000
Net Worth	$59,000
Total Monthly Income	$4,600
Total Monthly Expenses	$2,850
Monthly Cash Flow	$1,750

This outline gives a comprehensive diagram of your money related wellbeing, making a difference you make educated choices around budgeting, sparing, and overseeing obligation.

By displaying your money related assessment in a table arrange, you will be able effortlessly survey and get it your monetary wellbeing. This organized approach makes it easier to recognize regions for change and track your advance over time.

By taking after these steps, you will assess your monetary circumstance precisely and lay the groundwork for compelling budgetary administration. Routinely upgrading this assessment will assist you remain on track and accomplish your budgetary objectives.

CHAPTER II

ESTABLISHING A BUDGET

Making a budget is fundamental for overseeing your funds viably. This chapter will direct you through the steps to make a successful budget, present diverse budgeting strategies, and give cases of budget formats.

Steps to create an effective budget

Step 1: Determine your income

Calculate your total monthly income from all sources, including salary, freelance work, rental income, and any other earnings.

Example:

Income Source	Monthly Amount
Salary	$3,500
Freelance Work	$500
Rental Income	$600
Total Monthly Income:	**$4,600**

Step 2: List your expenses

Categorize your expenses into **fixed** and **variable expenses**.
- **Fixed expenses** are those that remain constant each month, such as rent, mortgage, and insurance.
- **Variable expenses** fluctuate monthly, such as groceries, transportation, and entertainment.

Example:

Expense Type	Monthly Amount
Fixed expenses	
Rent/Mortgage	$1,200
Utilities	$150
Insurance	$200
Loan Payments	$400
Total Fixed Expenses	**$1,950**
Variable expenses	
Groceries	$400
Transportation	$150
Entertainment	$100
Dining Out	$150
Miscellaneous	$100
Total Variable Expenses	**$900**
Total Monthly Expenses	**$2,850**

Step 3: Set budgetary objectives

Recognize your short-term and long-term money related objectives. Short-term objectives may incorporate paying off credit card obligation, whereas long-term objectives might include sparing for a down installment on a house or retirement.

Example:

- **Short-term Goal**: Pay off $2,000 credit card debt in 6 months.
- **Long-term Goal**: Save $20,000 for a home down payment in 5 years.

Step 4: Create a budget plan

Allocate your income towards your expenses and goals. Ensure that your total expenses do not exceed your income.

Example:

- Income: $4,600
- Expenses: $2,850
- Remaining Income: $1,750
- Savings/Goals Allocation:
    - Emergency Fund: $500
    - Credit Card Debt Repayment: $300
    - Retirement Savings: $400
    - Home Down Payment Savings: $550

Step 5: Track and adjust your budget

Screen your investing routinely and compare it to your budget. Make alterations as vital to remain on track.

Utilize devices like spreadsheets, budgeting apps, or a devoted budgeting note pad to assist track your accounts.

Budgeting methods

50/30/20 BUDGET

This method allocates 50% of your income to needs, 30% to wants, and 20% to savings and debt repayment.

Example:

- **Needs (50%)**: $2,300 (rent, utilities, groceries)
- **Wants (30%)**: $1,380 (entertainment, dining out, hobbies)
- **Savings/Debt Repayment (20%)**: $920 (savings, debt payments)

ZERO-BASED BUDGET

In this method, every dollar of your income is designated for a specific purpose, ensuring that you allocate all funds by the end of the month.

Example:

- **Income**: $4,600
- **Expenses + Savings + Debt Repayment**: $4,600
- **Remaining Balance**: $0

ENVELOPE SYSTEM

Allocate cash for different spending categories into envelopes. Once an envelope is empty, you cannot spend any more in that category for the month.

Example:

- Groceries: $400 in cash
- Dining Out: $150 in cash
- Entertainment: $100 in cash

Examples of budget templates

Basic Monthly Budget Template

Income		Expenses	
Salary:		**Fixed Expenses**	
Freelance Work:		Rent/Mortgage:	
Other Income:		Utilities:	
Total Income:		Insurance:	
Savings/Goals		Loan Payments:	
Emergency Fund:		**Total Fixed Expenses:**	
Debt Repayment:		**Variable Expenses**	
Retirement Savings		Groceries:	
Other Goals		Transportation:	
Total Savings/Goals:		Entertainment:	
Total Expenses:		Dining Out:	
Remaining Income:		Miscellaneous:	
		Total Variable Expenses:	

- **Total Expenses**: The sum of fixed expenses plus variable expenses
- **Remaining Income**: The result of subtracting the sum of Total Expenses and Total Savings/Goals from the Total Income.

Detailed budget template

Income Sources		Monthly Expenses	
Primary Job		**Housing**	
Side Hustles		Rent/Mortgage	
Investments		Property Taxes	
Other		Home Insurance	
Total Income		**Utilities**	
		Electricity	
		Water	
		Gas	
		Internet	
		Phone	
		Transportation	
		Car Payment	
		Gas	
		Public Transit	
		Maintenance	
		Food	
		Groceries	
		Dining Out	
		Insurance	
		Health Insurance	
		Auto Insurance	
		Life Insurance	
		Debt Repayment	
		Credit Card	
		Student Loan	
		Other Loans	
		Savings	
		Emergency Fund	
		Retirement	
		Specific Goals	
		Miscellaneous	
		Entertainment	
		Hobbies	
		Personal Care	
		Miscellaneous	
		Total Expenses	

Annual budget template

Annual Income		Annual Expenses	
Salary		**Housing**	
Freelance Work		Rent/Mortgage	
Investments		Property Taxes	
Other		Home Insurance	
Total Annual Income		**Utilities**	
		Electricity	
		Water	
		Gas	
		Internet	
		Phone	
		Transportation	
		Car Payment	
		Gas	
		Public Transit	
		Maintenance	
		Food	
		Groceries	
		Dining Out	
		Insurance	
		Health Insurance	
		Auto Insurance	
		Life Insurance	
		Debt Repayment	
		Credit Card	
		Student Loan	
		Other Loans	
		Savings	
		Emergency Fund	
		Retirement	
		Specific Goals	
		Miscellaneous	
		Entertainment	
		Hobbies	
		Personal Care	
		Miscellaneous	
		Total Expenses	

CHAPTER III

EFFECTIVE SAVING TECHNIQUES

Sparing cash is not close to cutting back on costs; it is embracing vital approaches that maximize your reserve funds potential. Whether you are sparing for a blustery day, a major buy, or long-term money related security, this chapter will prepare you with commonsense strategies and bits of knowledge to construct a strong establishment of reserve funds.

From month to month sparing techniques to shrewd investing propensities and comparison-shopping tips, you will find significant steps to optimize your budgetary wellbeing and accomplish enduring monetary opportunity.

Monthly saving methods

Sparing cash on a month-to-month premise requires teach and a clear technique. Here are a few viable strategies:

- **Automate Your Savings**: Set up programmed exchanges from your checking account to an investment funds account right after you get your paycheck. This guarantees you spare some time recently you spend.
- **50/30/20 Rule**: This well-known methodology proposes distributing 50% of your wage to needs, 30% to wants, and 20% to savings and investments.

- **Weekly Saving Challenge**: Increment your investment funds incrementally each week. For illustration, spare $1 within the first week, $2 within the moment week, and so on. By the conclusion of the year, you will have spared a critical sum.

Reducing unnecessary expenses

Cutting down on unnecessary expenses is crucial for effective saving. Here are some strategies:

- **Track your spending**: Keep a detailed record of your daily expenses. This helps identify where your money is going and highlights areas where you can cut back.
- **Eliminate subscriptions you do not use**: Cancel memberships and subscriptions that you rarely or never use, such as gym memberships, streaming services, or magazine subscriptions.
- **Avoid impulse purchases**: Implement a waiting period for non-essential purchases. For example, wait 24 hours before buying something you want. Often, the impulse will pass, and you will decide you do not need the item.

Smart shopping techniques

Being a smart shopper can significantly reduce your monthly expenses. Here are some tips:

- **Create shopping lists:** Always shop with a list to avoid buying items you do not need. Stick to the list to prevent impulse buys.

- **Price comparison:** Compare prices across different stores and online platforms before making a purchase. Use price comparison apps and websites to find the best deals.
- **Buy in bulk:** For non-perishable items, buying in bulk can save you money overall. Ensure you have the storage space and will use the items before they expire.
- **Use coupons and discounts:** Take advantage of coupons, discount codes, and sales. Look for deals in newspapers, online, and in-store flyers.

By implementing these effective saving techniques, you can manage your finances better, reduce unnecessary expenses, and increase your savings each month.

CHAPTER IV

MAINTAINING AND ADJUSTING THE BUDGET

Creating a budget is the first step, but ensuring its effectiveness requires ongoing attention and flexibility. This chapter will guide you through the process of regularly monitoring your financial progress, making necessary adjustments, and staying adaptable to life's unexpected financial challenges.

You will learn how to track your spending, identify areas for improvement, and make informed decisions that keep you on track with your financial goals. By mastering the art of budget maintenance and adjustment, you will be better prepared to navigate financial uncertainties and achieve long-term stability.

Tracking progress

Checking your monetary advance is pivotal to guarantee that your budget is working successfully. Here is how to do it:

- **Regular reviews:** Set aside time each week or month to survey your budget. Check your investing against your budgeted sums and alter as vital.

- **Use financial tools:** Utilize budgeting apps and computer program to track your costs and salary in real-time. Devices like Mint, YNAB (You Wish A Budget), or spreadsheets can offer assistance keep your accounts organized.
- **Record keeping:** Utilize budgeting apps and computer program to track your costs and salary in real-time. Devices like Mint, YNAB (You Wish A Budget), or spreadsheets can help keep your accounts organized.

Periodic budget adjustments

Budgets are active and ought to be balanced intermittently to reflect changes in your budgetary circumstance. Here is how to create those alterations:

- **Monthly reviews:** At the end of each month, review your budget and compare it to your actual spending. Identify any discrepancies and adjust your budget for the following month accordingly.
- **Quarterly adjustments**: Every three months, take a deeper look at your finances. Assess any changes in your income, expenses, or financial goals. Adjust your budget to accommodate these changes.
- **Annual revisions**: At the conclusion of the year, conduct a comprehensive audit of your budgetary circumstance. Assess your advance towards your monetary objectives and make fundamental alterations to your budget for the up-and-coming year.

Managing Financial Emergencies

Unexpected financial events can disrupt even the most carefully planned budgets. Here is how to manage such situations:

- **Emergency fund**: Maintain an emergency fund that covers at least three to six months' worth of living expenses. This fund provides a financial cushion during unexpected events such as job loss, medical emergencies, or urgent repairs.
- **Reprioritize spending**: Within the occasion of a budgetary crisis, reassess your budget and prioritize fundamental costs. Cut back on non-essential investing to free up reserves for the crisis.
- **Seek assistance**: Do not hesitate to seek help if you need it. This could be in the form of financial advice from a professional, temporary loans from family or friends, or exploring government assistance programs.

By frequently following your advance, making occasional alterations, and having a arrange input for money related crises, you will be able guarantee that your budget remains compelling and versatile to your changing budgetary needs. This initiative-taking approach helps you remain on track together with your money related objectives and gives peace of intellect knowing merely are arranged for startling challenges.

CHAPTER V

TIPS AND TRICKS TO MAXIMIZE SAVINGS

Whereas sparing cash can some of the time feel challenging, executing compelling procedures can altogether boost your reserve funds potential. In this chapter, you will find progressed sparing methods, keen speculation alternatives, and long-term monetary arranging strategies.

Whether you are looking to extend your month-to-month investment funds, make astute speculation choices, or arrange for future budgetary security, these down to earth experiences will enable you to optimize your money related wellbeing and accomplish your investment funds objectives more proficiently.

Advanced saving strategies

To maximize your savings, consider implementing these advanced strategies:

- **Increase savings rate**: Gradually increase the percentage of your income allocated to savings and investments. Aim to save a specific percentage of any windfalls or raises you receive.

- **Automated Savings:** Set up automated transfers from your checking account to your savings or investment accounts. Automating savings ensures consistency and reduces the temptation to spend.
- **Cut Down on Fixed Expenses:** Review your recurring expenses such as utilities, insurance, and subscriptions. Negotiate better rates or switch to more cost-effective options to free up more money for savings.

Basic investments to boost savings

Investigate these essential speculation choices to develop your reserve funds:

- **High-Yield savings accounts**: Consider opening a high-yield investment funds account that gives superior intrigued rates than conventional reserve funds accounts. These accounts are low-risk and give liquidity.
- **Certificates of Deposit (CDs)**: CDs offer higher interest rates than savings accounts but require you to lock in your money for a specific period. They are ideal for savings you do not need immediate access to.
- **Index funds**: Contribute to list reserves, which are a broadened portfolio of stocks that track a particular list. They offer wide advertise presentation and potential for long-term development.

Long-Term financial planning

Plan for your financial future with these long-term strategies:

- **Retirement planning**: Start contributing to retirement accounts such as a **401(k)** or **IRA** as early as possible. Take advantage of employer-matching contributions and tax benefits to maximize your savings.
- **Education savings**: Open a **529 savings plan** or other education savings accounts to save for future education expenses for yourself, your children, or other family members.
- **Estate planning**: Create or update your will, designate beneficiaries for accounts, and consider setting up trusts to manage and protect your assets for future generations.

By applying these tips and traps, you will upgrade your investment funds technique, investigate fundamental speculation openings, and lay the basis for a secure monetary future. Arranging ahead and making informed monetary choices nowadays will assist you accomplish your long-term budgetary objectives tomorrow.

CONCLUSION

In conclusion, "**The Art of Saving: How to Budget and Save Money Each Month**" has given profitable experiences and down to earth procedures to enable you in overseeing your accounts viably. All through this book, we have secured basic perspectives of money related administration, from understanding your current monetary circumstance to setting up and keeping up a budget that works for you.

Key Takeaways

- **Understanding your finances:** We explored the importance of assessing your income, expenses, and financial goals. This foundational step sets the stage for effective financial planning.
- **Budgeting techniques:** You learned various budgeting methods such as the 50/30/20 rule and zero-based budgeting, each designed to help you allocate your income wisely and achieve financial stability.
- **Effective saving strategies:** From automating savings to cutting unnecessary expenses, we discussed practical strategies to increase your savings rate and achieve your financial objectives faster.
- **Investment basics:** Basic investment options like high-yield savings accounts and index funds were introduced to help you grow your savings over the long term.

- **Long-Term financial planning:** We emphasized the importance of planning for retirement, education, and estate management to secure your financial future.

Last words of support

As you set out on your money related travel, keep in mind that budgetary victory could be a slow handle that requires dedication and discipline. By actualizing the techniques and procedures laid out in this book, you are taking proactive steps towards money related opportunity and security.

Share your advance

We empower you to share your encounters, victories, and challenges with others. By trading information and supporting each other, we are able all accomplish our money related objectives more successfully.

Thank you for choosing "**The Art of Saving**" as your direct to money related strengthening. May your travel towards monetary wellness be fulfilling and satisfying.

ADDITIONAL RESOURCES

Past the methodologies and strategies examined in this book, these assets offer extra direction to upgrade your budgeting and sparing endeavors. You will discover budget and investment funds layouts to streamline your money related arranging, as well as suggestions for apps, books, and courses to develop your monetary education. Moreover, we propose our "**Bill Tracker Notebook**," a fundamental apparatus for overseeing your bills and costs productively. Utilize these assets to remain educated, organized, and enabled as you work towards accomplishing your budgetary objectives.

Additional budget and savings templates

To further support your financial planning efforts, here are additional budget and savings templates you can utilize:

- **Monthly budget template**: A point-by-point layout to track your month-to-month wage and costs, permitting you to designate stores successfully over distinct categories.
- **Savings goal tracker**: Set and screen your investment funds objectives with this tracker, making a difference you remain propelled and on track towards accomplishing money related points of reference.
- **Debt payoff plan**: Utilize this format to strategize and track your advance in paying off obligations, counting credit cards, credits, and other liabilities.

- **Emergency fund calculator**: Calculate how much you would like to spare for crises based on your month-to-month costs and wanted security net.
- **Investment portfolio pracker**: Screen the execution of your ventures, counting stocks, bonds, and common stores, to survey development and make educated choices.

Additional budget and savings templates

Monthly budget template

Category	Budgeted Amount	Actual Amount	Difference
Income			
Salary	$3,000	$3,200	+$200
Freelance	$500	$450	-$50
Total Income	**$3,500**	**$3,650**	**+$150**
Fixed Expenses			
Rent/Mortgage	$1,200	$1,200	$0
Utilities	$150	$140	-$10
Insurance	$200	$200	$0
Total Fixed Expenses	**$1,550**	**$1,540**	**-$10**
Variable Expenses			
Groceries	$400	$420	+$20
Transportation	$150	$160	+$10
Entertainment	$100	$90	-$10
Miscellaneous	$100	$80	-$20
Total Variable Expenses	**$750**	**$750**	**$0**
Savings/Goals			
Emergency Fund	$200	$200	$0
Vacation Fund	$100	$100	$0
Retirement Fund	$100	$100	$0
Total Savings/Goals	**$400**	**$400**	**$0**
Total Expenses + Savings	**$2,700**	**$2,690**	**-$10**
Remaining Income	**$800**	**$960**	**+$160**

Annual savings goals template

Savings Goal	Target Amount	Amount Saved	Amount Remaining	Deadline
Emergency Fund	$5,000	$2,500	$2,500	12/31/2024
Vacation Fund	$3,000	$1,500	$1,500	08/30/2024
Home Down Payment	$20,000	$10,000	$10,000	12/31/2025
New Car	$10,000	$3,000	$7,000	12/31/2024
Total Savings Goals	**$38,000**	**$17,000**	**$21,000**	

Debt repayment plan template

Debt Type	Total Amount Owed	Interest Rate	Monthly Payment	Remaining Balance	Payoff Date
Credit Card	$5,000	18%	$200	$4,800	06/2025
Student Loan	$20,000	5%	$300	$19,700	12/2030
Car Loan	$15,000	4%	$350	$14,650	12/2027
Personal Loan	$10,000	7%	$250	$9,750	12/2028
Mortgage	$150,000	3%	$1,200	$148,800	12/2040
Total Debt	**$200,000**		**$2,300**	**$197,700**	

* Interest is not considered

Weekly savings tracker template

Week	Amount Saved	Running Total	Notes
Week one	$50	$50	Saved from cutting dining out
Week two	$75	$125	Bonus from freelance work
Week three	$40	$165	Reduced grocery bill
Week four	$60	$225	Skipped movie night

Expense tracker template

Date	Description	Category	Amount	Payment Method	Notes
07/01/2024	Grocery Shopping	Groceries	$100	Credit Card	Weekly groceries
07/03/2024	Electric Bill	Utilities	$75	Debit Card	Monthly bill
07/05/2024	Gasoline	Transportation	$50	Cash	Weekly fuel
07/07/2024	Dining Out	Entertainment	$30	Credit Card	Dinner with friends

Bill tracker template

Bill Type	Due Date	Amount Due	Amount Paid	Payment Date	Notes
Rent	07/01/2024	$1,200	$1,200	07/01/2024	Paid via bank transfer
Electric Bill	07/05/2024	$75	$75	07/04/2024	Paid online
Internet Bill	07/10/2024	$60	$60	07/09/2024	Paid via credit card
Car Payment	07/15/2024	$350	$350	07/14/2024	Paid via direct debit

Net worth tracker template

Asset Type	Value	Liability Type	Amount Owed	Net Value
Home	$200,000	Mortgage	$150,000	$50,000
Car	$20,000	Car Loan	$10,000	$10,000
Savings Account	$5,000	Credit Card	$1,000	$4,000
Investments	$15,000	Personal Loan	$5,000	$10,000
Total Net Worth	**$240,000**		**$166,000**	**$74,000**

We also recommend acquiring our "**Bill Tracker Notebook**", which provides ample space and organization for recording bill payments and managing your finances efficiently. This comprehensive tool complements the strategies discussed in "**The Art of Saving**" and enhances your financial planning toolkit.

Printed in Great Britain
by Amazon